THE MEANINGS OF MODERN ART

by JOHN RUSSELL

Art Critic, *The New York Times*

VOLUME **4**

REALITY REASSEMBLED

THE MUSEUM OF MODERN ART, NEW YORK

I. Pablo Picasso, *Les Demoiselles d'Avignon*, 1907
The Museum of Modern Art, New York

Copyright © 1974 by The Museum of Modern Art   All rights reserved   Library of Congress Catalog Card Number 72-76416
Series ISBN 0-87070-477-X   Volume Four ISBN 0-87070-481-8   Designed by Earl Tidwell
Cover: plate XII. Georges Braque, *Café-Bar*, 1919. Kunstmuseum, Basel

In the art of this century one painting has a place apart: Pablo Picasso's *Les Demoiselles d'Avignon*, 1907 (pl. I).

This in a way is odd; for the *Demoiselles* is not a masterpiece in the old, outright, unarguable sense. By the standards of Raphael or Poussin or Ingres it could even be called a failure. Picasso himself seems never to have regarded it as finished but simply to have turned its face to the wall and got on with other things. It was not seen in public until 30 years after it was painted.

Yet there is no doubt that the *Demoiselles* is the white whale of modern art: the legendary giant with which we have sooner or later to come to terms. It was always, and it is still, a demanding picture. It is an edgy, scary, almost a dislikable picture. It awes, but it does not seduce. And yet seduction is, on one level, what the *Demoiselles* is all about: seduction of a blatant and demystified kind but seduction nonetheless.

The scene is the parlor of a turn-of-the-century whorehouse in Barcelona. The basic subject is one common enough in Old Master painting: beauty on parade. The Old Masters used most often a mythological pretext: the Temptation of St. Anthony, Susannah and the Elders, Diana and Callisto. Above all they used the Judgment of Paris: nothing in the Latin poets was more advantageous for the Old Masters than the moment at which Paris said "Goddesses, undress!" when he was called upon to decide whether Venus, Juno or Minerva was the best-looking. No one has ever had a better visual memory than Picasso, and he would certainly not have forgotten what Rubens, for one, had made of that subject (fig. 1). When he came to paint the *Demoiselles* the three girls on the left were just as Rubens had placed them in the version of *The Judgment of Paris* which is now in London, and the two figures on the right were just as Rubens had placed his Paris and his Mercury: almost too close, all this, for coincidence.

In several of his first sketches for the *Demoiselles* Picasso introduced some clothed male figures: patrons of the house, for whose benefit the parade was being mounted. But in the painting itself the latter-day Paris and the latter-day Mercury were both played by women. The Paris figure glares round at us in a veritable ecstasy of connivance; the Mercury figure parts the curtains, the better to see what is going on. In any enclosed society—ship at sea, barracks, prison camp—the inmates take an intense pleasure in masquerades which distract them from the routines of everyday; and Picasso in the *Demoiselles* shows how the five girls keep boredom at bay. Not only do they reenact their daily task at an exalted level, but they even have on the table before them the legendary apple which Paris will award to the goddess of his choice.

Picasso knew such houses from his years in Barcelona. He was old enough to have verified the prognosis which had been given to him in a palm-reading when he was still a boy: that where women were concerned he would be imperious in his choices and quick to act upon them. Degas and Toulouse-Lautrec had proved that life in a brothel could be endowed with an offhand, lapsed grandeur that had nothing to do with conventional titillation. Yet there remained the fundamental question: how to restate all this in modern terms? How to "make it new" in a way which would be true to him, Pablo Picasso, in the 26th year of his existence, and true to the needs of art in the winter of 1906–07? How to take the future by the throat?

Picasso had in mind the epic scale which Matisse had lately attempted in such pictures as his *Joy of Life* (Volume 2). Cézanne's *Grandes Baigneuses* (Volume 1) was the measuring rod for all such enterprises at that time, and as the *Demoiselles* developed it turned out that the composition was anchored by a squatting figure derived from the woman in the lower right-hand corner of the *Three Bathers* by Cézanne (Volume 2) which belonged to Matisse. But meanwhile the first drawings for the *Demoiselles* suggested an easygoing linear design with no overtones of emotional stress: a party of pleasure, in fact, set down in calligraphic terms. As entries in a diary, these first drawings would have been ideally lively; but as drafts to be enlarged on the scale of epic they lacked something of monumentality. Doubtless it was to put this right that in a later draft Picasso penciled in, almost unchanged, the majestic, sculptural *Two Nudes* (fig. 4) which he had finished painting not long before.

These nudes were very different from the adolescents, delicate and androgynous, whom he had been painting as recently as the summer of 1906. Anatomies too fragile for the traffic of life were replaced by bodies that seemed about to sink into the ground beneath their own weight. Skins as tender as the paps of a dormouse were replaced by what looked like an outcrop of reddish-brown stone. Buttocks fit for a baby elephant were seen in low relief. Breasts and forearms had a monumental life of their own. Heads were colossal, deep hewn and suggestive of anything but feminine frailty. The fastidious, allover play of light that had caressed the human body and given it an ideal harmony had quite vanished. Light and dark were now in the artist's gift, to be granted or taken away at will; and there was something willful and disjunctive about the way in which parts of the body had been put together. The open, shelving backgrounds of the Rose Period gave way in the *Two Nudes* to a narrow ledge and to what looked like a heavy curtain perhaps six inches behind the two giantesses.

1. Peter Paul Rubens
The Judgment of Paris, c. 1632–35
The National Gallery, London

2. Pablo Picasso
Study for "Les Demoiselles d'Avignon," c. 1907
Kunstmuseum, Basel

At the stage represented by this pencil and pastel sketch, the
Demoiselles still looked as if it might shape up, in the end, like
a traditional group photograph in which one or two people
happened to have taken their clothes off. The two clothed
men, in particular, have an air of unconcern which is quite
absent from the painting.

4

3. Pablo Picasso
Woman Combing Her Hair, 1906
The Museum of Modern Art, New York

From the winter of 1905–06 onward Picasso's development accelerated to such a degree that quite often, as here, he combined three or four modes of utterance within a single painting. In the head of the *Woman Combing Her Hair* the influence of ancient Iberian sculpture is as strong as it is in its contemporary, the portrait of Gertrude Stein (fig. 19). The torso has still something of the tender particularity of the bodies of the Blue and Rose Periods; and the ill-defined but richly painted background is a souvenir of another phase in Picasso's evolution—that of the figure groups of 1905–06.

These were figures on an epic scale. Cézanne had been mated with Iberian sculpture to produce the first of the elemental women who were to be in and out of Picasso's work for many years to come. But although the figures in epic may well be larger than life in physical terms, they should be larger than life in moral terms also; and there should be something of superhuman energy in their articulation. The *Two Nudes* were not right for the *Demoiselles,* and the scene as drawn had neither bite nor bounce; Picasso did not carry it further. Trial and error persuaded him in time to change what had begun as a kind of convivial group photograph into something more angular, more briskly energized. The relaxed curvilinear style of the earlier drawings dropped out of sight; elbows and knees were poised like missiles ready for firing; bodies were shown in vigorous action; draperies, table and still life echoed the tusky, arrowy, sharp-pointed forms which Picasso had stressed throughout the rest of the design. In what now seems to us the final draft, he introduced a more dynamic version of the left-hand figure in the *Two Nudes;* thereafter, he was ready to go.

He had second and third thoughts, even so, while actually painting the picture. In fact it may almost remind us today of the façade of St. Mark's in Venice, so freely and with such abandon did Picasso loot the art of other times and other places for whatever suited his purpose. He manifested in this the stylistic imperialism which is one of the marks of advanced art in this century. As much as T. S. Eliot in the last section of *The Waste Land* or Ezra Pound in the *Cantos,* Picasso in the *Demoiselles* has a pivotal position in time. The picture carries the future within it, but it also carries the past. It has echoes and adaptations of Iberian sculpture, Egyptian art, El Greco, Cézanne and African sculpture, as well as more general affinities with Old Master painting. It also may be said to comment upon the more recent past. It could, for instance, be called the last great Symbolist painting, so heavy is its load of powerful and yet ambiguous subject matter. And it could be called the most haunting of all Expressionist paintings, such is the wrench it gives to all preexisting notions of the expressive potential of the human body. No great painting sits more squarely on the hinge of time.

Throughout the *Demoiselles* Picasso continually shifts his ground as far as visual conventions are concerned. The ever-increasing intensity of the subject matter was paralleled by the mounting complexity of the picture language. What had begun as a Cézannesque parade of beauty ended up as what the art historian Leo Steinberg has called "a tidal wave of female agression." Correspondingly, what had begun as a figure subject to be rendered in harmonious and unified style ended as a dismantling

4. Pablo Picasso
Two Nudes, 1906
The Museum of Modern Art, New York

of a tradition that had ruled since the Renaissance. On both levels the picture was bound to be profoundly disturbing. The women had distinctly got out of hand: there is something in the *Demoiselles*—not much, but something—of the haplessness with which the male faces the female in Munch. But what is borne toward us on that tidal wave is not, in the last resort, a domineering professional sexuality. It is *the future,* made visible. That is why the *Demoiselles* so dismayed the few friends of Picasso who were allowed to see it. It marked the end of something, and his friends could read it only in terms of privation and loss.

In that respect we are in a privileged position. We know that the *Demoiselles* was not only "the end of something." It was also the beginning of Cubism, a movement as fruitful as any in the history of art: between the year 1909 and the outbreak of World War I, Picasso, Braque and Juan Gris produced an almost unbroken succession of supremely beautiful pictures. It also opened up, incidentally, a whole new range of possibilities for sculpture. The *Demoiselles* did not lead immediately to Cubism, for the ideas within it were too many and too complex for even Picasso himself to exploit all at once. But if Cubism had from 1909 onward a developmental energy which never fails to astonish us, much in that is owed to the proving ground of the *Demoiselles.* Alfred H. Barr in his pioneering study of Picasso (*Picasso: Fifty Years of His Art,*1946) refers to the *Demoiselles* as "a transitional picture, a laboratory or, better, a battlefield of trial and experiment"; and no one could better this description of a painting which, though in many ways still enigmatic and self-contradictory, will never cease to straddle history like a colossus.

"*Les Demoiselles d'Avignon* may be called the first Cubist picture," said Mr. Barr, "for the breaking up of natural forms, whether figures, still life or drapery, into a semi-abstract all-over design of tilting, shifting planes compressed into a shallow space is already Cubism." No less fundamental to Cubism is the combination, exemplified above all in the squatting figure on the right, of several points of view within a single image. There is, on the other hand, little trace in fulfilled Cubist painting of the epic scale, the raunchy subject matter, the hectic emotional tone or the heterogeneous inspiration of the *Demoiselles:* these traits were peculiar to Picasso at a certain moment in his evolution.

HISTORY AND HAPPENSTANCE

A further legacy of the *Demoiselles* was the unquestioned freedom to reorder the evidence of sight. This, once again, was fundamental to Cubism. It is perhaps at this point that we should try to distinguish those characteristics of the initial phase of Cubism which were in the personal gift of Picasso or Braque from

5. Pablo Picasso
Head, 1906
The Museum of Modern Art, New York

One of the earliest of the individual sketches which can be related to the *Demoiselles* is this *Head* in watercolor. In its introspective and atmospheric quality, with eyes downcast and the shape of the head adjusted to an elegant and elongated oval, the little picture looks back to the stylish melancholy of Picasso's Blue and Rose Periods, as well as forward to the *Demoiselles*.

6. Pablo Picasso
Head of a Man, 1907
The Museum of Modern Art, New York

By the spring of 1907 Picasso was feeling his way toward a more and more arbitrary way of treating the components of the human head. This was to find its fullest expression in the two right-hand figures in the *Demoiselles*; but meanwhile, as here, he asserted his right to assemble the features of the face as and how he pleased, and to turn the shadow of the nose into a series of African-type striations up and down the right cheek.

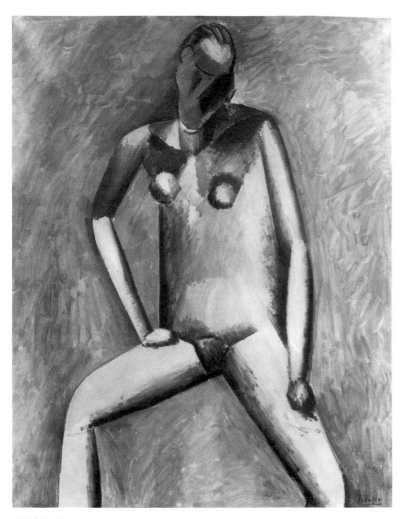

7. Pablo Picasso
Seated Nude Woman, 1908
Philadelphia Museum of Art

those other, more general dispositions which were part of the climate of the age. This is a matter in which the emphasis can easily fall the wrong way. Picasso and Braque were the co-founders of Cubism; and they ridiculed the idea that there was any real correspondence between what they had done and what now seems to us a comparable achievement in other departments of human effort. If pictorial space changed its character at the same time as the physicists were revising our notions of physical space, that was simply coincidence. If our notion of matter as something solid and unchanging was revolutionized just as Picasso and Braque were revolutionizing the presentation of solid objects in art, that was another coincidence. Cubism as developed by them was in their view a purely intuitive art, based on the detached and objective contemplation of subject matter which was for the most part both commonplace in itself and emotionally neutral. They were in tune with the times to the extent of having a boyish admiration for pioneer aviators like Wilbur Wright; but as for Einstein and Max Planck and Ernest Rutherford and Niels Bohr, they had never so much as heard of them.

No one disputes this. But it is also true that we are influenced in our ideas, in our outlook and in our behavior by people we have never heard of. Matisse wrote in 1933 that "our senses have a developmental age which is not that of our immediate environment, but that of the period into which we were born. We are born with the sensibility of that period, that phase of civilization, and it counts for more than anything that learning can give us." Picasso painted the *Demoiselles* at a time when civilization was identified to a considerable extent with the ideology of scientific progress—with the idea, in other words, of a triumphal advance toward a firmer grasp of the conditions of modern life. In one field after another, human frailty was to be eliminated and age-old commonsense convention overthrown. What did Max Planck single out in 1908 as the essential factor in the development of theoretical physics? "A certain emancipation from anthropomorphic elements, and especially from specific sense-impressions." What did the philosopher Edmund Husserl wish to substitute in 1907 for the sumptuous mix of memory and association on which Marcel Proust, for one, had nurtured his gifts? What he called a "phenomenological reduction": an ascetic method of apprehending objects which would arrive quickly and surely at their essence. All this was in the air; and Cubist painting relates to it even if the Cubist painters did not. Cubist painting is central not only to the art of this century but to much of the thought of this century as well. A great Cubist painting ideally illustrates, for instance, the point made not long ago by Jean Piaget, founder of the psychology of intelligence, when he said that it was essential to distinguish between "knowledge as a copy and knowledge as an assimilation of reality." In Cubism, as much as in Piaget, reality is "seen to consist of a series of transformations beneath the appearance of things. In order to know objects," Piaget goes on, "we have to act on them, to break them down, and to reconstruct them."

Knowledge as a copy has no place in Cubism. But we have to deal here with a most delicate equipoise of internal contradictions. It is true that Picasso and Braque set out from 1909 onward to look at objects simply and straightforwardly, without predetermined notions of what they were like. Everyone agrees that their intentions were what is called "realistic." Courbet was evoked by the poet Guillaume Apollinaire and others as the true father of the Cubists, on the grounds that he too—in his still lifes, above all—had set out to demystify painting. Certainly he aimed at a matter-of-fact, no-nonsense approach; but what emerges from his monumental mounds of apples and pears is, even so, the nobility and generosity of Courbet's own temperament. Objectivity loses out in the end, and we are left not with the matter-of-fact but with a human statement unique for its rich, slow beat and the steadfastness of its underlying beliefs.

In Cubism, equally, we discover in the end that what seemed important at the time—the "rational," "scientific," "objective" element—resulted in large degree from an act of self-deception on the part of sympathizers who wished to apply to Cubism the names then most in favor. If those names went on being applied to Cubism, it was in part because reproductions of Cubist painting emphasize the "rational" or "scientific" aspect of the work. What gets left out of even the best reproduction is the wayward, often hesitant and in any case quite unscientific pressure of the brush as it touches the canvas more or less lightly with a load of paint that is more or less heavy. There are paintings by Picasso and Braque from the years 1910–11 which look in reproduction to be armored against our scrutiny; but when we come face to face with the originals we find that on the contrary they are sanctuaries of openheartedness in which nothing is kept back from us.

For the founding fathers of Cubism did not aim to create a kind of art for which any preexisting name was appropriate. Their object was to define the terms on which painting could survive in a changed world. Reason and objectivity played their part in this, and so did "science" of a sort. But if Cubism can be said to have saved the dignity and the coherence of painting at a time when those characteristics were in jeopardy, much in that was owed to nonscientific qualities also: imagination, for one, and deep feeling, for another, and truth to self, for a third.

8. Georges Braque
Large Nude, 1907–08
Private collection, Paris

9

II. Georges Braque
Road near L'Estaque, 1908
The Museum of Modern Art, New York

III. Pablo Picasso
*Still Life with Bread and Fruitdish on a
    Table*, 1909
Kunstmuseum, Basel

It is an indication of the dynamic of
Picasso's career that the year 1909, which
produced such fidgety, prismatic Cubist
paintings as the *Still Life with Liqueur
Bottle* (fig. 10) should also have prompted
the *Still Life with Bread and Fruitdish* on
a *Table*. Everything here seems larger,
grander and more stable than in everyday
life. The majesty of the hinged table, the
bare, strong outline of the bread, the total
lack of fuss or histrionics—all relate back
to the ancient traditions of Spanish still-life
painting; it is as if, after the agitations of
the *Demoiselles*, Picasso had come
through to the kind of calm, clear, exact
statement which proves all over again that
absolute dignity can characterize the
furniture of life.

9. Pablo Picasso
Big Dryad, 1908
The Hermitage Museum, Leningrad

Cubism arose from the notion—and whether it was entirely true is irrelevant—that art was in the doldrums; or, at any rate, that it had far too much unfinished business on its hands. The problems posed by Cézanne were fundamental to the continuance of serious art; nobody had dealt with them in ways which had a general application. It was common ground with many people that single-point perspective had become a hindrance to art; nobody had found a principle of internal organization which could take its place. Cézanne had had no equal in the portrayal of solid forms, but he had achieved this by conceptualization after a very long series of individual acts of perception; the equilibrium involved in this was personal to himself. Cézanne had introduced into his paintings a most delicate spatial ambiguity by what in French is called *passage:* the running together of planes which in the picture space are far apart, so that the old notions of foreground and background are dissolved in a tautly constructed planar structure. This likewise had implications as yet undeveloped.

Other, more general problems remained open. There was the notion of the flatness of the picture surface, so clearly formulated by Maurice Denis in 1890 in a famous article called "A Definition of Neo-Traditionism" and yet so difficult to put into practice; that flat surface so often looked inert and decorative. There was the problem of color; since Gauguin everyone had known that color should be set free, but by the winter of 1906–07, when Picasso began to hatch out the *Demoiselles,* it looked as if color had not so much been liberated as turned loose with nowhere to go. Altogether, painting was in deep trouble. On the one hand, much was expected of it: a new age called for a new art, and people at such times feel personally let down, if not actually disgraced, if art does not do what they ask of it. On the other hand, art was manifestly being relieved of many of its traditional functions. A young painter, Fernand Léger, summed this up in 1913 when he wrote that technology had put a lot of art out of business. "How can Salon painting compete," he asked, "with what is available today in every cinema in the world? Each of the arts today is isolating itself and limiting itself to its own field." The function of Cubism, in this context, was to serve as a redoubt—an unassailable fortress for an irreducible art.

Van Gogh had said not long before he died that in future the great steps forward in art would be undertaken collectively, since no one man could be strong enough to bear the burden. He was borne out in this by the history of Cubism, which was from its beginnings a joint operation. Picasso and Braque were its cofounders. It was a partnership of opposites, but it was also a partnership of equals. From time to time their contemporary Fernand

Léger worked in ways tangential to theirs; and from 1912 onward a young painter, Juan Gris, continued the movement with an authority and a coherence which were distinctly his own. But fundamentally Cubism was the invention of Picasso and Braque. In its reverberation—in the extent, in other words, to which it made the future possible—their alliance was akin to that of Bertrand Russell and A. N. Whitehead, who at much the same time were producing, in *Principia Mathematica,* a complete deductive system, based on a very few first principles, which laid the foundation of modern logic and led in time to the development of the computer system. Cubism was not "a system," in that sense, but it was an achievement of comparable stature.

Georges Braque had been introduced to Picasso by Apollinaire toward the end of 1907. The friendship was slow to develop, and in background and character the two men could hardly have been more different. Picasso had a fine-art inheritance—his father was for many years a professor in the Barcelona Academy of Fine Arts—and in his first youth he was already the coming man in one of the most sophisticated cities in Europe. Braque, in contrast, was the son and grandson of professional housepainters. The height of ambition in his family had been to become a prosperous master craftsman. By the year 1899 Picasso knew what was going on in art all over Europe, whereas Braque was a sedulous apprentice in the provincial city of Le Havre, learning how to plaster, how to paint and paper a wall, how to simulate the textures of fine wood and rare marble. His was a relatively dull and limited milieu, and even when he finally got to paint full-time in Paris his outward progress was slow. Yet it was Braque, alone among Picasso's friends, who made sense of the *Demoiselles* after a first instinctive revulsion; and it was Braque, in the summer of 1908, who came back from the little town of L'Estaque, near Marseilles, with what were later called "the first truly Cubist paintings."

Picasso, meanwhile, had found it difficult to follow the *Demoiselles.* He tackled one after another the formal inventions which had been made to cohabit in that great and terrible painting; but there was an evident and painful sense of stress in many of the pictures which resulted. He was like an engine which is so powerful that no chassis yet developed can house it; and from time to time there were paintings like the *Big Dryad* of 1908 (fig. 9) which gave off an almost palpable sense of elemental energies for which no definitive use had been found. It was at this point that Braque with his composed and impregnable nature and his steady, consistent methods of work began to play an ever larger part in Picasso's life. Braque had for some time been awed by the beauty and dignity of Cézanne's achievement; L'Estaque was a

10. Pablo Picasso, *Still Life with Liqueur Bottle,* 1909
The Museum of Modern Art, New York

Something of the difference between Picasso and Braque comes out in the contrast between these two paintings (figs. 10 and 11). If the Braque is more broadly and generally conceived, it is more a matter of generous forms generously modeled, and if it has touches of much higher color, that may be in part because it is the earlier picture of the two and because Cubism was not yet so distinctly based on sharp-edged, prismatic planes and near-monochromatic color. But there is something peculiar to Picasso in the use of idiosyncratic objects like a many-faceted bottle of Spanish anisette, which is in the lower left-hand half of the painting, and the rather less legible ceramic bottle in the form of a cock which is above and to the right of it. Picasso had by this time proceeded much further toward the adoption of an all-purpose, prismatic form—like a folded sheet of writing paper, which paces the image and determines the speed at which information is given to the observer—and it is already quite difficult to read the individual objects in the picture.

IV. Pablo Picasso
Woman with Pears, 1909
The Museum of Modern Art, New York

This painting and the bronze *Woman's
Head* (fig. 16) are sister images—
reworkings of a shared idea. In the
bronze, the twist of the neck and
shoulders gives the whole sculpture a
specific impetus: a turning motion
which is echoed by the general direction of the deeply shadowed angular
planes of the head. In the painting,
Picasso has modeled the outline of the
left shoulder and the left side of the
neck, right up to the back of the left
ear, in terms of a continuous, girder-like
form which tilts over to the left as it
reaches the level of the cheekbone.
This offsets the many broken, sharp-
angled and deftly tilted forms which
make up the right side of the head; and
both idioms are echoed in turn by the
draperies, the fruit on the table, the
tablecloth and the table itself. The
integration of these many types and
varieties of form into a single, completely harmonious and fully expressive
composition is one of the major
achievements of Picasso's career before
1914.

14

V. Georges Braque
Man with a Guitar, 1911
The Museum of Modern Art, New York

11. Georges Braque
Still Life with Fruit, 1908
Nationalmuseum, Stockholm

apt, since there are no cubes in Cubist painting, but it stuck. One column-inch in a newspaper dated November 14, 1908, established Braque as the pioneer of the movement; and as he went on his ruminative way he produced a still life in late 1908 (fig. 11) in which intersecting planes were dramatized by the quite arbitrary fall of the light, and early in 1909 a harbor-scape (fig. 12), painted in Paris, which was fundamental to the development of Cubism. The memory of Cézanne still presides over it; the repeated triangles which form up in the sky, the sails of the boat on the left and the detailing of the jetty are related to the lofty, echoing, triangular forms in the *Grandes Baigneuses.* But Braque had evolved on his own a method of unifying the painting by causing the sky, the sea, the boats, the lighthouses and the harbor itself to run on into one another—each coaxing the other, as it were, to take over the burden of structuring the picture. Braque's ambition was to remake space in such a way that each object would come forward in turn—to be stroked, almost, as antelopes are stroked in a zoo. (The art historian John Golding says of the *Harbor in Normandy* that "the optical sensation produced is comparable to that of running one's hand over an immensely elaborate, subtly carved sculpture in low relief.")

In the preface which Apollinaire wrote for Braque's first one-man show at Kahnweiler's, in November, 1908, he rightly singled out the element of "angelic moderation" in Braque's nature. But to be angelic is not to be characterless; Braque in 1908–09 defined the immediate ambitions of Cubism in a way that testified to the operation of a most powerful and resourceful intelligence. "Angelic" remains the right word, however, for the final effect of Braque's early Cubist work, which is that of a peaceable kingdom of forms, each of which submits with total docility to its presentation in a continually changing space. That kind of thing was quite foreign to Picasso's nature, and when in the summer of 1909 he produced his first group of completely realized Cubist paintings they had quite another character. Alike in landscape and in portraiture, he displayed a powermindedness and a drive toward total possession which were quite absent in Braque.

Picasso was undoubtedly stimulated by the fact of being in Spain, at Horta de San Juan. Gertrude Stein made one of her more helpful remarks when she said that "in the landscapes which he painted there he emphasized the way of building in Spanish villages, the line of the houses not following the landscape but cutting across and into the landscape, becoming indistinguishable in the landscape by cutting across the landscape. . . . The color too was characteristically Spanish, the pale silver yellow with the faintest suggestion of green, the color afterwards so well known in Picasso's cubist pictures. . . ."

favorite workplace of Cézanne's, and had Braque been an everyday "follower of Cézanne" he would have seized, in that summer of 1908, on the first facts about the landscape there, which were the devouring brilliance of the light and the saturated blue of the sky. But in fact he did nothing of the kind. The landscapes which he brought back with him were filled with a hooded light of his own devising. In their compositional scheme the sky played no part. They were severe, tightly constructed paintings in which color was restricted to the most sober of greens and ochres. Contours were broken, contrasts of "near" and "far" were often contradicted, forms opened up into one another, and houses were splayed out in such a way that more was seen of them than could have been seen from any one point of view in life.

A SHARED RESPONSIBILITY

It was with respect to these paintings that the critic Louis Vauxcelles wrote that Braque "reduces everything—places, figures, houses—to geometrical schemas, to cubes." The name was never

12. (*far left*) Georges Braque
Harbor in Normandy, 1909
The Art Institute of Chicago

13. (*left*) Georges Braque
*La Roche-Guyon: the
    Château*, 1909
Nationalmuseum,
Stockholm

14. (*below left*)
Pablo Picasso
Factory at Horta de Ebro,
    1909
The Hermitage Museum,
    Leningrad

15. (*below*)
  Pablo Picasso
Houses on the Hill, Horta,
    1909
Private collection,
    New York

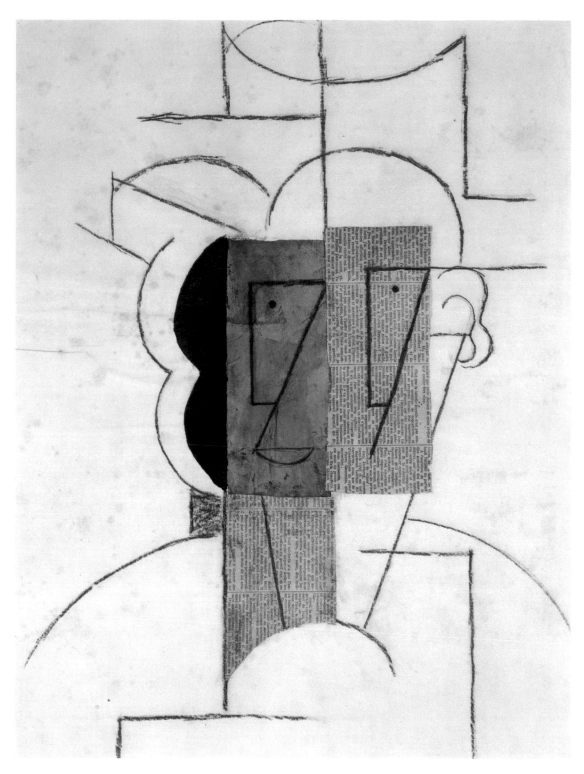

VI. Pablo Picasso
Man with a Hat, 1912
The Museum of Modern Art, New York

It was fundamental to Synthetic Cubism that color and form could act independently of one another. In other words, color was not required to describe, or even to identify form. In *Man with a Hat* there is a progression from light to dark as we read the head from right to left. The newsprint, now discolored with age, stands for the cheek which faces the light; the rich blue stands for the shadowed center of the face; the ink-black section to the left stands for those parts of the head which are in darkness and might not even be seen in normal conditions. Austere and summary as the drawing may be, there are signs that Picasso, the master portraitist, has been at work. Looks and character are defined in telegraphic form and we can see that the derby hat has come from the best English makers. More than one scholar has lately pointed out that the printed matter was not chosen at random but includes apt references to tuberculosis, in the text that marks the location of the man's upper chest, and to nostrils and teeth in the text that runs vertically past his mouth and nose.

16. Pablo Picasso
Woman's Head, 1909
The Museum of Modern Art, New York

17. Pablo Picasso
Girl with a Mandolin, 1910
Private collection, New York

Spain did something for Picasso: physically, in that he identified far more strongly with its spare, bleached landscapes than with the green distances of northern France, and morally, in that his ideas suddenly began to pull all the same way and with redoubled force. Nothing in earlier painting quite prepares us for the pounce on the essentials of form which Picasso achieved at Horta de San Juan. There was something in this of the sculptural interests which had come out so strongly in the *Demoiselles:* each form was given a specific vibration, a throb all its own, which would not have been found, or permitted, in the more conciliatory universe of Braque.

Picasso retained, however, his polyvalent curiosity. His work

18. (*left*)
Pablo Picasso
Portrait of Leo Stein,
   c. 1905
Philadelphia Museum
   of Art

19. (*below*)
Pablo Picasso
Gertrude Stein, 1906
The Metropolitan Museum
   of Art, New York

20. Pablo Picasso
Portrait of Ambroise Vollard, 1909–10
Pushkin Museum, Moscow

During his long life (1867–1939) Ambroise Vollard was the champion, the dealer and often the confidant of more than one generation of great painters. With his secretive and contrary nature, he was not easy to deal with; but it was he who arranged Cézanne's first retrospective exhibition in 1895, and Bonnard, Vuillard, Picasso, Braque, Chagall and Rouault were among the artists to whom he gave important commissions.

21. Pablo Picasso
Female Nude, 1910–11
Philadelphia Museum of Art

language, on the one hand, and the demands of human particularity, on the other. A prize instance of this is the portrait of the dealer Ambroise Vollard, which Picasso painted in the winter of 1909–10 (fig. 20). The surface of the painting is densely articulated in terms of a consistent, closely networked series of small, intersecting planes. This structure is independent of the contours of Vollard himself and of the still life which accompanies him; yet we have no difficulty in recognizing traits familiar to us from other likenesses of Vollard—the high-domed skull, the redoubtable knob of flesh at the end of the nose, the slight downward twist at the corner of the thin lips, and the deceptive air of being half asleep.

In the summer of 1910 Picasso once again returned to Spain, to be rewarded by another important step forward in his art. The basic element in the pictorial architecture was thereafter no longer the closed, sculptural form which had survived, in however multifaceted a manner, until then. It became something quite different: a linear framework made up, in the case of a figure painting, of the outlines or main directional lines of the body. This framework was used as the basis for a system of open, blade-like planes which intersected with one another, forming an autonomous structure that sometimes referred to the human figure and at other times went its own way. We can see from the *Female Nude* now in Philadelphia (fig. 21), done at Cadaqués in the crucial summer of 1910, that although these paintings are not easy to decipher they have a presence as formidable as anything in the *Demoiselles*.

Picasso did not want to produce cult objects which would be accessible only to the few. Nor did he want to go over the edge and produce paintings which were purely abstract. He wanted to go on painting pictures which *presented* the visible world but did not *represent* it; he wanted to be sure that an intelligent person who looked at those pictures would know what he was looking at; at the same time he wanted to retain and enrich the new formal language which he and Braque had evolved. Between the autumn of 1910 and the spring of 1912 they worked on this problem. Picasso solved it by introducing a system of visual cues which gave the observer a broad hint as to what was going on. Fragments of reality were imported complete into the picture—a watch chain, the name of a newspaper, a carpenter's T square, a calling card, the tassel from an upholstered armchair—with the object of forcing the observer to interpret the pictorial structure in terms of the known world and not merely as a structure which had its own internal consistency and existed in and for itself.

With Picasso these cues never quite lost the character of a challenge. It was man against man as he baited and needled the

was still full of echoes and allusions, and full also of contradictory ambitions within one and the same picture. The *Girl with a Mandolin* (fig. 17), painted in Paris early in 1910, is in feeling a throwback to the elegiac figure painting of the Rose Period; parts of the body are modeled with a fullness and a tender simplicity which look back to the work of five years earlier, but at the same time Picasso has stamped the head flat on the picture plane. Picasso was still working from the model with the kind of tenacity which Cézanne had displayed in front of his sitters; and where the look of his sitters is known to us we can estimate how strong was the tension between the demands of the evolving picture

22. Georges Braque
Still Life with Violin and Jug, 1909
Kunstmuseum, Basel

In life, the violin and the jug would have stood squarely on the table. But in Braque's picture space is tipped up and forward and everything in it—violin, jug, table, dado, angled wall, nail on that wall—is brought up close to us. Front, back and sides are seen simultaneously; and what in life would move sedately away from us comes alive in an elaborate system of hinges and flaps and diamond-edged facets that is nearer to El Greco's giddying *View of Toledo* than to the sobriety of conventional still life. Only the nail is true to everyday vision: partly in irony, partly to show that old ways of seeing can be combined with the new, and partly as a visual pun, to suggest that the picture is itself hung on that same wall.

23. Georges Braque
The Portuguese, 1911
Kunstmuseum, Basel

observer into identifying the subject of the picture. Braque was, as always, less combative in his approach. But he put the important questions all the same. Already in the winter of 1909–10 he inserted a perfectly legible illusionistic nail, complete with shadow, into the great still life called *Still Life with Violin and Jug* (fig. 22). The point of this was twofold. First, it took the picture out of the esoteric, fine-art world by suggesting that it had been nailed to the wall as a flat, painted surface of no particular consequence. Secondly, it was a reminder of the alternative convention: centuries old picture-making methods, based on the imitation of everyday experience. In the spring of 1911 Braque introduced an idea of much wider and more lasting significance when he stenciled the letters BAL at the top of *The Portuguese* (fig. 23), a single-figure painting prompted by the memory of a musician he had seen in a Marseilles bar. Like the nail, the letters served to remind the observer of other and more familiar ways of conveying information. But, unlike the nail which had only one function, they were versatile adjuncts which could fulfill a wide variety of purposes. Weightless and incorporeal, they had a firm, exact, unalterable shape and substance; in this, they contrasted with the painted surface of the picture and made the observer conscious all over again both of the two-dimensional nature of the painted surface and of the three-dimensional forms which were being presented. And they could be read, finally, as they are read in life, for a specific message.

They signaled, in other words, a change of pace. A new kind of scrutiny was called for; and this at a time when the dosage of verifiable fact in Cubist painting was much diminished. "At the time," Picasso said to William Rubin, the art historian, when discussing a painting done in the spring of 1912, "everyone talked about how much reality there was in Cubism. But they didn't really understand. It's not a reality you can take in your hand. It's more like a perfume—in front of you, to the sides. The scent is everywhere, but you don't quite know where it comes from." Lettering introduced a new kind of specificity into painting; looking at Cubist painting in sequence, we realize that until that point it was deeply conservative in many of its aspects. The half-length seated figure, the neutral materials of still life, the landscape that kept close to the motif: all these were the classic constituents of European art. Cézanne, Corot and Chardin (above all with his *Attributes of the Arts*) stood godfathers to Cubist painting between 1908 and 1912. The paintings were real paintings, handmade with brush and pigment; and even at their most audacious they still have—or so it seems today—an Old-Masterly echo. It is Rembrandt, against all expectation, who comes to mind when we look afresh at the tenebrous frontal *Female Nude* which Picasso painted in Cadaqués in that summer of 1910.

The importation of lettering, as a ready-made, nonhandpainted element, was therefore a considerable step. With his craftsmanly upbringing and his extreme sensitivity to substance, Braque was anxious in 1912 to get away from the severe and all but monochromatic procedures which Cubism had developed since 1910.

24. Pablo Picasso
"Ma Jolie" (Woman with a Zither or Guitar), 1911–12
The Museum of Modern Art, New York

If not too much of life, then at any rate too much of language was excluded by those procedures. The new formal vocabulary could never have been developed if color had not been exiled; but the exile hurt, all the same. It is always a moving moment when we

23

26. Pablo Picasso
The Architect's Table, 1912
The Museum of Modern Art, New York

25. Georges Braque
Still Life with Ace of Clubs, 1912–13
Musée National d'Art Moderne, Paris

In this picture Braque reworked, in terms of oil paint and charcoal drawing, the ideas which he had used in the first of his pasted-paper pictures some six months earlier. To make the earlier picture he had bought a roll of wallpaper which had been printed to simulate oak paneling. He cut three strips from this paper in the shapes that he wanted and stuck them down to represent, respectively, two sections of wood paneling and the drawer of a table. Next, he drew across them in such a way that they became equal partners with the charcoal drawing of grapes, a glass, and the words BAR and ALE that made up the rest of the picture. In the painting reproduced here, Braque used his decorator's comb to simulate wood-graining. What had been done with real paper in September, 1912, was here imitated, in other words. With its taut construction, its ruthless flattening of volumes which till recently would have been shown in full three-dimensional style, and its further ramming home of the point by the use of objects which are in themselves flat—like the playing cards and the folded newspaper—this painting is one of the masterpieces of Synthetic Cubism.

watch color being sent off, as it were, in the great still lifes which Braque painted in the winter of 1909–10; and now the delicate thing was to reintroduce it without allowing it to reintroduce illusionistic space—for such is our conditioning that we simply cannot see two patches of colored pigment side by side without reading them in spatial terms. Somehow, color had to be brought back on quite another basis.

THE INVENTION OF COLLAGE

It was brought back toward the end of 1912 as part of a new development which was of enormous and lasting importance for 20th-century art. Braque and Picasso had been pondering for months whether it would be possible in future to *build* their pictures, as much as to paint them. Braque would seem to have been, in this, the logician who said, "If we want to show a man reading a newspaper, why do we have to fake it up with brushes and oil paint when we could just as well get the newspaper itself and stick a bit of it on the canvas?" This flouted both the Puritan ethic of hard work and the trade-unionism of the trained *artiste-peintre*; but it made good sense. Picasso tried something of the sort early in 1912, when he introduced into one of his still lifes a piece of oilcloth which had been overprinted to simulate chair caning; and in September, 1912, Braque went into a shop in Avignon, bought a length of artificially wood-grained wallpaper, and used it with perfect congruity to indicate the drawer and top of a wooden table on which were assembled the classic elements of Cubist still life: a glass, a fruit dish, a bunch of grapes, and the words BAR and ALE.

It was characteristic of the difference between the two men that Picasso's first steps in collage were direct and overtly subversive, as he thickly over-painted part of the oilcloth in order to lock it down into the substance of the painting. Braque by contrast introduced his strips of wood-grained paper in an exploratory way (figs. 27 and 28). Picasso's textures were so dense as to force the observer almost to rub his nose in the picture to find out what was going on; Braque's had plenty of air blowing through them. In a matter of months Picasso was using the new medium with a quite extraordinary freedom and élan, as if relishing every moment of the new and total liberty which he and Braque had brought into painting. For painters—"picture-builders" might be a better name—were now free to make their pictures from whatever materials took their fancy. They were also free to change the identity of those materials, and to use them literally, as themselves, or metaphorically, or in a purely formal compositional way and with no reference to their identity in the world from which they had been lifted.

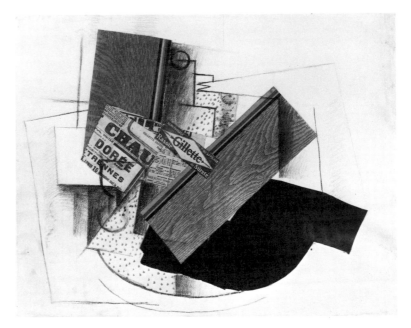

27. Georges Braque
Still Life on a Table, 1912
Private collection, Paris

28. Georges Braque
Still Life (with word "Vin"), 1913
Philadelphia Museum of Art

25

VII. Juan Gris
Breakfast, 1914
The Museum of Modern Art, New York

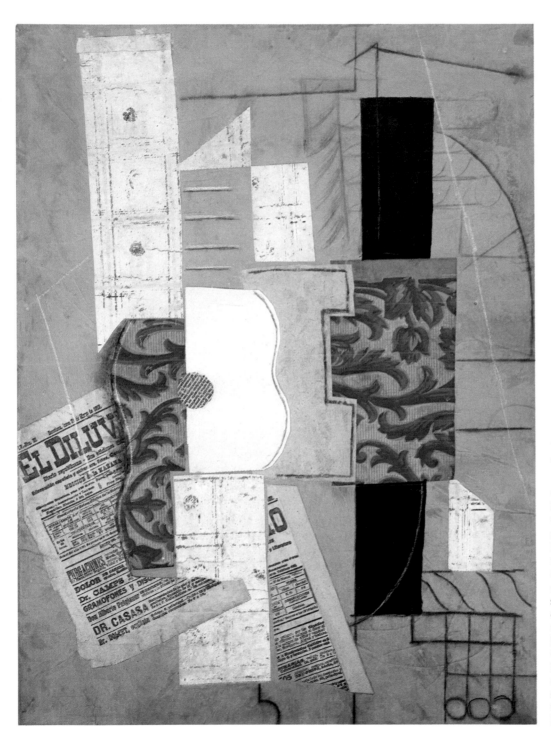

VIII. Pablo Picasso
Guitar, 1913
Private collection, New York

Guitar is on one level a formal statement marked by particularly strong contrasts of color and texture. It is also a storehouse of allusions, not all of them easily deciphered. Picasso has always been a master of the verbal joke that may or may not pass unnoticed, and those who can read the small print in *Guitar* will find once again a wealth of sly insinuation. Even the round sound-hole of the guitar secretes a printed echo of the "lengthy ovations" which had been given to a speaker who upheld the "principles of liberty." Those principles are vindicated, in *Guitar*, by the freedom and assurance with which Picasso lays down a grand general design, on the one hand, and on the other hand pencils in such almost clandestine references as the fringed tassels which hang (bottom right) from the braided arm of a chair.

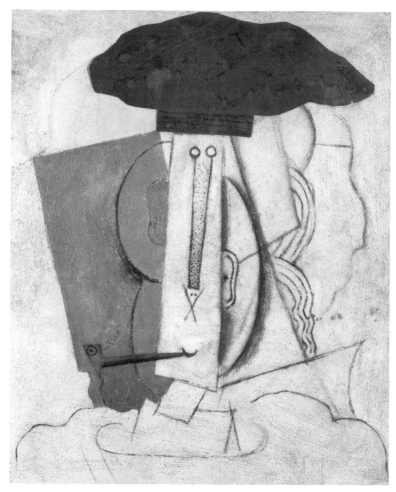

29. Pablo Picasso
Student with a Pipe, 1913–14
Private collection, New York

30. Pablo Picasso
Fruit Dish, 1909
The Museum of Modern Art, New York

In one and the same picture Picasso would, for instance, use a piece of newspaper and a fragment of sheet music as themselves; he would indicate the outline and texture of a guitar with four pieces of pasted paper, one of which was wood-grained (and therefore suggestive of the guitar's appearance in life) whereas the other three were not; and he completed the picture with a drawing of a wineglass which was complete in itself, had been drawn on a separate piece of paper, dated from a year or two earlier, and was in short not so much a drawn glass which was integral to the picture as a drawing of a glass which was also a historical object. In pictures of this sort identities were changed, ignored, borrowed or unexpectedly kept intact in ways which

have never lost their capacity to surprise us. Color was employed as a free agent, without reference to modeling or light. The strips of colored paper were flat by their very essence—so much so that when they were drawn over, as they often were, there was no temptation to identify the drawn form with color beneath it. All this brought into painting a new kind of physicality: one that was clear, open and lean. Not only the painting itself but the act of looking at it was restructured; and there was as much an increase in the pleasure given, and in the kinds of pleasure involved, as there was in the material possibilities which were henceforward at the painter's disposal.

Picasso played in all this the more vigorous role. It amused him

31. Pablo Picasso
The Violin (Violin and Compote of Fruit), 1913
Philadelphia Museum of Art

32. Pablo Picasso
Guitar and Wineglass, 1913
Marion Koogler McNay Art Institute, San Antonio, Texas

enormously, for example, to parody his own labors of a year or two before. Insolence (in Alfred Barr's phrase) was added to paradox when the subject matter of the *Fruit Dish,* done in early spring, 1909 (fig. 30), turned up in his *Violin and Compote of Fruit* of 1913 (fig. 31), in the form of some colored illustrations of apples and pears, cut out of a book, with newsprint and plain white paper to indicate the dish. Yet the new experience was as complete and as enriching as the earlier one. And although Braque in general was not so aggressive in his use of the new medium, he did not disdain its opportunities for comedy. One of the grandest of his pasted-paper works is also one of the few

in which no musical instrument appears. But what is it that anchors the whole composition in place? A rectangular strip of paper, cut from the title of a pulp novel, on which one word appears complete: VIOLON.

In 1912 Picasso and Braque were reinforced by the emergence of Juan Gris as a painter of real importance. Gris had been living in the same building as his compatriot Picasso since shortly after he arrived in Paris in 1906, at the age of nineteen. He had therefore been ideally placed to watch the progress of Cubism from the days of the *Demoiselles* onward. He had not presented himself as an aspiring painter but rather as a clever and attentive

33. Juan Gris
Rooftops, 1911
The Solomon R.
    Guggenheim Museum,
    New York

34. Juan Gris
The Man in the Café, 1912
Philadelphia Museum of Art

Put on view in October, 1912, only a few months after Gris had made his debut as a painter, *The Man in the Café* impressed at once by its size, its assurance and its schematic presentation of the given subject. The strict linear framework operated, in fact, as a kind of mincing and flattening machine from which nothing was allowed to escape.

young man from out of town who lived by making illustrations for the humorous papers. His background was in the exact sciences—mathematics and engineering—and when he did begin to paint, in 1911, he tackled the problems one by one, in his own way, and made no attempt to rush the preliminaries. There was nothing fudged or approximate about his early paintings, and when he first showed his pictures, in October, 1912, they impressed at once by their almost military command of any given situation. In the portrait of Picasso, 1912 (fig. 35), for instance, the fall of the light was plotted as if promotion at West Point depended upon it. In the second half of that year he developed a way of picture building in which the color was bright and high and a rigorous linear diagram parceled out the canvas; each particular parcel was then allotted to a sectional view of the subject matter (see fig. 34). Sometimes these sectional views were realistic, sometimes they weren't; Gris kept his options open. Trained as he was to keep a given subject in mind in all its mathematical aspects, he was able to plot his pictures in advance in a way that would never have appealed to the more intuitive Picasso and Braque. When he applied himself to extending the pasted-paper technique, in 1914, he did it with characteristic thoroughness.

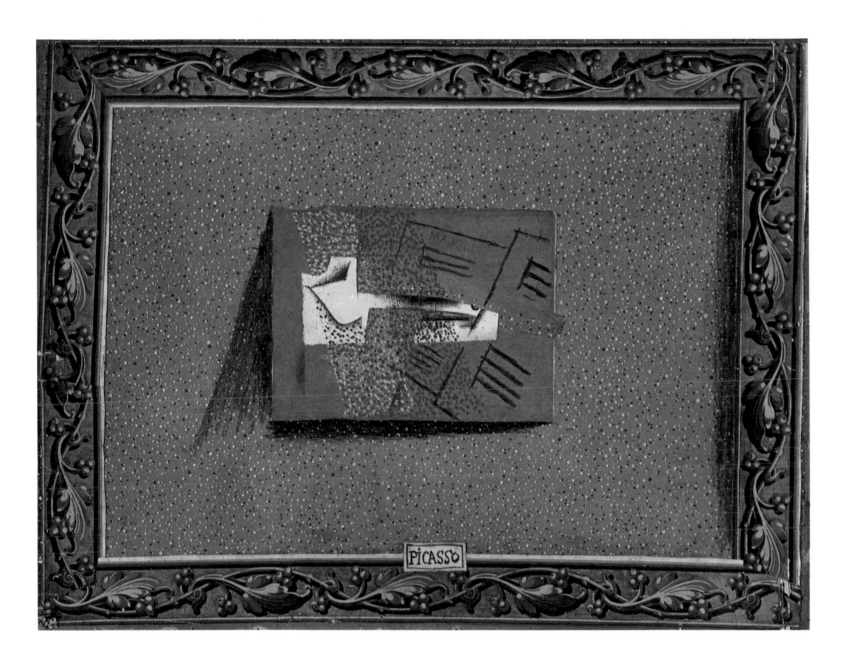

IX. Pablo Picasso
Pipe and Musical Score, 1914
The Museum of Fine Arts, Houston, Texas

Picasso by 1914 was able to elaborate the surfaces of his pasted-paper works until the picture became a kind of total environment: an arena for wit and fancy of all kinds, in which Picasso would begin with a painted surround for the image proper, add a frame of his own invention and end with a simulated name-plate at the point where a proud collector might wish to put PICASSO in big letters. Gertrude Stein claimed later that for much of this there was a precedent in Picasso's native country: "In the shops in Barcelona instead of postcards they squared little frames and inside it [*sic*] was placed a cigar, a real one, a pipe, a bit of handkerchief, etcetera, all absolutely the arrangement of many a Cubist picture and helped out by cut paper representing other objects. That is the modern note that in Spain has been done for centuries."

35. Juan Gris
Portrait of Picasso, 1912
The Art Institute
of Chicago

36. Juan Gris
Grapes and Wine, 1913
The Museum of Modern Art, New York

Instead of using the papers in a dispersed and intermittent way, he allowed them to cover the whole, or almost the whole, of the canvas in accordance with a preestablished formal idea. This idea often operated quite independently of the subject matter to be presented; color was likewise left free and had not, as a rule, any descriptive function. From that point onward he allowed the subject matter to make its way into the picture, much as a latecomer in a crowded train finds a seat as best he can.

But just as there is usually someone who gets off the train at the next station, so Gris allowed for a give-and-take at this stage between the initial design and the nature of the subject matter. Gris by 1914 was a master organizer; there is creativity of a cool but quite special kind in the exactitude with which he would cut and trim his papers to the nearest fraction of an inch, and in the agility with which he would combine and recombine point after point of precise circumstantial detail. In the final product we see realized the dream of a world in which everything is ordered, everything is known, and everything finds expression in the clearest and most logical way. Once again, the act of looking is restructured as we realize with what a variety of lucid statement Juan Gris has presented the traditional still-life material.

Nor is there any doubt that Gris was quite consciously defining the terms of an irreducible art: one whose privileges could be neither withdrawn nor counterfeited. *"On ne truquera plus les œuvres d'art"* ("There'll be no more faking of works of art") is

32

37. Juan Gris
Violin and Engraving, 1913
The Museum of Modern Art, New York

Gris had made a very close study of Cubist painting as it was practised by
Picasso and Braque, and he certainly knew the painting of 1909–10 in which
Braque had introduced a *trompe-l'œil* nail in what was otherwise a purely
Analytical Cubist picture. In *Violin and Engraving* Gris not only painted in a nail
of this sort but he pasted part of a real engraving into the frame in the upper
right half of the picture. He also introduced Braque's favorite subject matter,
the violin, while keeping to his own compositional device of building up the
picture in terms of tall, vertical strips offset by sharply pointed triangular forms.

38. Juan Gris
Playing Cards and Glass of Beer, 1913
The Columbus Gallery of Fine Arts, Columbus, Ohio

In *The Man in the Café* (fig. 34) the layout of the subject—its profile in space,
in other words—was much as it is in life. But by 1913 Gris was dividing his
canvas, as here, into vertical strips, within which the fragmented subject matter
was allowed not only to slide up and down, as suited the composition best,
but to be shown alternately in a naturalistic way and in notional form, as an
outline drawn on a ground of flat color. Gris had also developed a voluptuous
textural sense which delighted in the juxtaposition of many different kinds of
surface, from simulated marble to the smoothness of a real playing card, and
from patterned wallpaper to the rich, painterly substance of the foaming beer.

X. Fernand Léger
Contrast of Forms, 1913
The Museum of Modern Art,
  New York

In 1913 Léger painted a series of
pictures which were exactly what
their generic title suggests: contrasts
of forms. The contrasts in question
were as direct as possible—flat
shapes set off by forms which were
like sections cut from a drum. Léger
drew them in outline with the
unequivocal black line which was
the mark of his open and candid
nature; and he colored them with
bright reds, blues and yellows. Léger
prided himself on the punch which
was packed by these alliances of
simplified forms; but in a matter of
months he decided to return to
declarative statements which involved the traditional subject matter
of French painting (see *Village in
the Forest,* fig. 42).

39. Juan Gris
The Tea Cups, 1914
Kunstsammlung Nordrhein-Westfalen, Düsseldorf

40. Pablo Picasso
Still Life with Fruit, 1915
The Columbus Gallery of Fine Arts, Columbus, Ohio

41. Fernand Léger
Table and Fruit, 1909
The Minneapolis Institute of Arts

Léger was deeply impressed by the Cézanne memorial exhibition of 1907. In no way an opportunist, he took a long time to adjust to the experience; but eventually, as here, he began to work toward an emphatic personal statement of what it means to site fully realized forms in space. At this point he virtually abandoned color, the better to concentrate on the definition of form.

one of the printed messages on a picture dated 1914; another pasted-paper of the same year makes a sly reference to a new law which forbade the pasting of bills on public buildings; and in case we should forget the name of the man who has brought the whole thing about, we are allowed to see just four letters of the main headline of the newspaper on the table in *Breakfast,* 1914 (pl. VII): GRIS. What impresses in all this is the purity and coherence and consistency of Gris's ambitions and the strength of mind with which he carried them out. Psychologically his work does not have the layer upon layer of significance, and still less the ambiguity, which Picasso's never ceased to have. It would never have occurred to Gris, for instance, to combine two views of a guitar (as Picasso did in his *Guitar,* done in spring, 1913) in such a way as to make them into an emblem of a man and a woman making love; still less would he have allied this recondite image to a newspaper advertisement for "DR. CASASA, specialist in genital complaints." But there is a glorious openness and completeness about the way in which Gris had a specific idea of art and brought it to its point of maximum fulfillment.

As early as 1913 it was evident that the future of Cubism lay with the synthesization of objects: with the development, in other words, of a system of formal notation which would allow the painter to build a picture in terms of discrete elements and eventually to reassemble the subject matter in all its aspects. The pasted-papers did this with an effect of highspirited sophistication; they offer us the chance of taking part in a play-structure as subtle and as complex as can be found in art. It was a structure in which the promptings of instinct could be satisfied immediately: a sharp pair of scissors, and the thing was done. Flatness was literal flatness, and obvious to all; it no longer had to be worked for, against the associations of a lifetime and several centuries of handcrafting. Gris did marvels with the enclosed world of the pasted-papers; but the system which he proposed was, even so, a finite and self-referring one. There was no room in it for the violent and unresolved emotional impulses which Picasso had often to commemorate; and no room, either, for the undertow of deep feeling which Braque could create just by laying one piece of colored paper beside another. Picasso repeatedly overran the emotional frontiers of the pasted-papers, as Gris had established them, now raiding the terrain of Expressionism, now

42. Fernand Léger
Village in the Forest, 1914
Kunstmuseum, Basel

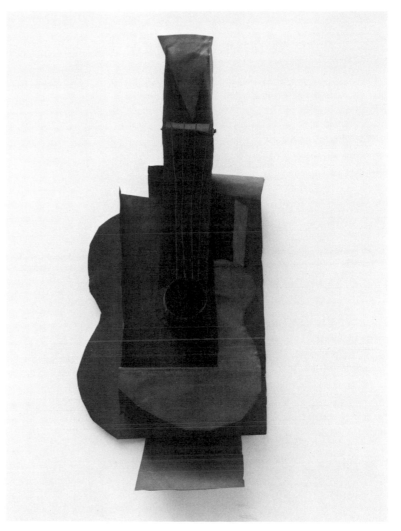

43. Pablo Picasso
Guitar, 1912
The Museum of Modern Art, New York

Léger here took a subject not unlike that of Braque's *La Roche-Guyon: the Château* (fig. 13). Braque muted the contrast between architecture and landscape and retained something of the feathery lightness with which Corot rendered nature in that same part of France. Léger, by contrast, gave an emphatic solidity to trees and houses alike, reducing the tree trunks to cylinders blocked out in a military red, foliage to a uniform, dark-shadowed egg shape, and houses to windowless canisters drawn in with an unwavering straight black line. The painting is as much a "contrast of forms" as any one of the paintings which actually bear that name, but the contrasts are tied to everyday reality.

Picasso's earlier sculptures (see the bronze *Woman's Head*, fig. 16) were conceived in traditional terms, as monolithic objects that could be seen from all sides. This *Guitar* is meant to hang on the wall, like a relief, and it treats the subject matter primarily in terms of flat shapes cut out of sheet metal and allowed to overlap in a shallow space. In this way the component parts of the guitar are not so much represented as *listed,* and the final product is not so much "a sculpture," in the 19th-century sense, as (to quote William Rubin) "a sculptural painting"—and even an anticipation of such paintings as the *Guitar and Wineglass* of 1913 (fig. 32).

44. Pablo Picasso
Glass of Absinth, 1914
The Museum of Modern Art, New York

45. Pablo Picasso
Still Life, 1914
The Tate Gallery, London

Toward 1914 Picasso began to make relief constructions—12 are known to survive—which are in effect three-dimensional extensions of the subject matter of his pasted-paper pictures. This *Still Life* is made of painted wood and its subject matter includes a wineglass (opened down the front and flattened into the wall behind it), an open sandwich, a knife, the round table to be found in so many Cubist paintings, a fringed tablecloth with tassels, and a strip of wall complete with dado. As a sculpture it is *built,* rather than modeled. The two slices of sausage, the handle of the knife, and the dado have been particularized with Picasso's characteristic offhand wit; but the historical importance of this *Still Life* lies in the new notion of sculpture which it promulgates. Sculpture is here set free from the unity of material which had persisted even in the metal *Guitar* of 1912 (fig. 43). From 1914 onward, intelligence was all.

racing ahead into what would later become the domains of Dada and Surrealism, now reinventing the whole notion of sculpture. It was, as I said earlier, as if in his case the engine were too big for the chassis; and as if he would have to revert one day to the heavier, slower and ultimately more consequential medium of oil paint on canvas. With Braque and Gris, he had shown that this was not the only medium in which serious pictures could be made; perhaps the time had come to carry over into the realm of

oil paint the gains which had been made with collage and pasted-paper?

For there is a moral quality about painting in oils. The marks on the canvas say something, in other words, about the person who makes them. The three Cubist masters knew this, and it was inevitable that they would turn back in the end to the medium in which they both challenged and continued the work of the Old Masters. What did Picasso say in 1923? "Drawing, design and

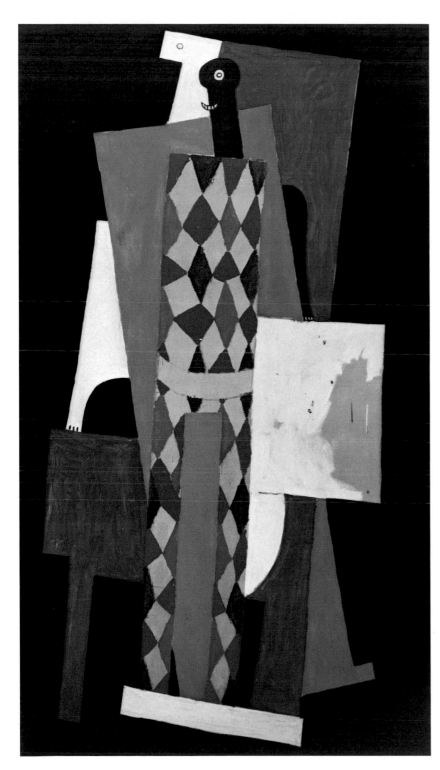

XI. Pablo Picasso
Harlequin, 1915
The Museum of Modern Art, New York

With this lifesized figure Picasso took a first long stride in the direction
of the epic representations of the human figure which were to abound
in his paintings of the 1920s. He also went further than ever before in
the systematic dislocation of the image of Harlequin—by giving us, for
instance, two quite separate views of the head and by redistributing his
arms, his trunk and his legs on many different levels and on planes
sharply distinct from one another. In complete and obvious contrast to
the sober monochrome of Analytical Cubism is the use in *Harlequin*
of the whole gamut of tonal oppositions, from bone-white to the deepest
of blacks, and from the classic festivity and precision of Harlequin's
costume to the enigma of the unfinished and barely brushed-in
rectangular form—a playbill, perhaps, or a sheet of music—which he
holds in his left hand.

46. Pablo Picasso, *Glass, Newspaper and Bottle*, 1914
The Museum of Modern Art, New York

47. (*left*) Pablo Picasso
Card Player, 1913–14
The Museum of Modern Art, New York

48. (*below*) Juan Gris
Still Life (Bottle and Fruitdish), 1917
The Minneapolis Institute of Arts

color are understood and practiced in Cubism in the spirit and the manner in which they are understood and practiced in all other schools." What did Gris say in 1921? "In practice I cannot break away from the Louvre. Mine is the method of all times, the method used by the masters." As for Braque, when he was invalided out of the French Army in 1917 and set down some of his thoughts about painting, he echoed the disciplines inherent in the French classical tradition. "Nobility comes from contained emotion," he wrote; "progress in art consists not in going further but in the knowledge of art's limits."

When oil painting once again took over the responsibility for Cubism, it was in a form suggested and sanctioned by the success of the pasted-papers. It made use, that is to say, of paper-thin planes superimposed one upon the other. There was virtually no illusion of space; the forms were flattened as if with a roller. Their presentation was varied by accents of bright color which would not have been seen in Cubism before 1912, and by variations of texture which derived from pasted-paper practice and are sometimes so elaborate as to constitute, as William Rubin has pointed out, "a *trompe l'œil* of collage." Between 1914 and 1916 Picasso was given to elucidating the position and extent of the overlapping planes with obtrusive patterning, with additions of sand to the paint and, on occasion, with verbal allusions of an esoteric sort. All these have their equivalent in the pasted-papers. Light and shadow did the rest.

This stage of Cubism was characterized by a certain evenmindedness of general effect. This was owed primarily to the ease and regularity with which the huge and readily distinguish-

49. Pablo Picasso
Guitar, 1919
The Museum of Modern Art, New York

Both Braque and Picasso produced, at the very end of the Cubist decade, major works in which the preoccupations of the previous ten years were given monumental and, in one way or another, definitive expression. Braque's *Café-Bar* (pl. XII) is one such; and this *Guitar*, another. Its point lies not so much in the guitar, painted on torn paper, which is attached to the canvas by two real and all but invisible pins, as in the tall, thin diamond which lies behind it. William Rubin argued in 1972 that the subject of the picture is not "a guitar," but a guitarist. The diamond-shape represents, in other words, an immensely simplified human figure, with just one or two very discreet clues as to its pose and location. Thus read, the picture would constitute a late if not final contribution to Cubist iconography. The use of a paper nail with a simulated shadow at the top of the guitar is an echo, also, of the ways in which nails were used in Cubist painting to point the difference between depicted reality and what we call in everyday speech "the real thing." Picasso in 1919, and in this picture, was able to use both of them simultaneously and in the same context.

XII. Georges Braque
Café-Bar, 1919
Kunstmuseum, Basel

It was after a long and slow convalescence that Braque returned to painting toward the end of World War I. In this seminal picture he applied the methods of "synthetic" or "late" Cubism to subject matter derived from popular life. The overlapping, flat planes defy conventional perspective and put us within touching distance of the basic elements of French café-life: the guitar, the sheet music, the white clay pipe on the table, the fruit in its dish, the diamond-patterned floor, the sharp-toothed decorative surround of door and window, the dado, the speckled wallpaper, the folded newspaper, the windowpane with its sprawly, outmoded lettering and the unpainted, rough-grained wood of the table. The lettering suggests that we are looking in from the street; but in reality we are neither inside nor out, but "in touch" with the scene in all its aspects. In its detail, the picture recalls the Cubist works of before 1914, with their stenciled letters and scraps of real newspaper; but in the majesty of its proportions, in the fullness and richness of its color, and in its ambiguous and equivocal exploration of space, *Café-Bar* looks forward to the symphonic interiors of 1939–55 which were to be the crowning glory of Braque's long career.

50. Georges Braque
Musical Forms (Guitar and Clarinet), 1918
Philadelphia Museum of Art

With the humblest possible materials and just a few pencil marks, Braque here creates one of the most sumptuous of his still-life images: a guitar, a clarinet, a piece of sheet music, a rectangular wooden table. *Musical Forms* is a farewell at six years' distance to the pasted-papers of 1912; but beyond the wit and concision of the formal statements there is a beauty of color that is peculiar to Braque—a combination of tans and ochres, pale yellow and rufous browns, which in earlier times would have called for a particularly resourceful use of the palette.

able flat planes seem to interlock in space, sliding back and forth beneath one another without let or hindrance. It was not an idiom in which there could readily be expressed anything approaching the violence or the agitation of the *Demoiselles.* Braque was supremely at home with it, and we shall see in a later Volume that Picasso in the summer of 1921 developed it still further in two festive masterpieces, versions I and II of the *Three Musicians.* But Picasso had not yet had the long experience of Diaghilev's Ballets Russes which went into the *Three Musicians;* nor was World War I the time at which to muster the all-pervading high spirits and the superabundant psychic energy which mark both variants of the work. More to the point, in the winter of 1915–16, was the gaunt figure of *Harlequin* (pl. XI), which Picasso set out against a void at a time of intense private emotional distress. In this painting he brought new starkness into Synthetic Cubism and reasserted, as so many times before and since, the elements of the sardonic and the undeceived within his complex nature.

I have in this Volume concentrated on Cubism itself as the creation of three men only. Insofar as there was a Cubist movement, it will be considered later; Cubism as a joint effort came to an end with the outbreak of World War I in August, 1914, and was never reintegrated. The friendship between Picasso and Braque had been too intense, and had been lived through at too great

an imaginative pressure, to be taken up again like a friendly game of chess. Phases in life cannot be relived, and when Braque came back from being trepanned in a military hospital his once-great strength had been diminished forever. But in his work of 1918–19 he produced what is in effect an elegy—and one of the most poignant things of its kind—for the lost oneness of the Cubist effort.

Picasso and Braque had not set out with any specific program in mind, and Picasso in 1923 rejected the idea of research in art with words which soon became famous: "To search is meaningless, in painting. To *find*—that is the thing." It will be clear from later Volumes that a very large proportion of what is best in this century's art has been predicated in one way or another on what Picasso and Braque "found" between 1907 and 1914. They had liquidated, one by one, the problems which had been left unsolved at the time of the death of Cézanne in 1906; they had given altogether new answers to the question, "What can a picture be?"; they kept alive the idea of the masterpiece and on many occasions lived up to it. In one sense, in 1914 their careers had hardly begun—certainly they were still giving new resonance to the idea of Cubism in the late 1940s and '50s—but it could equally be said that by the end of that fateful year they had completed what the art historian Edward Fry has rightly called the "greatest single aesthetic achievement of this century."

SUGGESTED READINGS

General

Breunig, LeRoy C., ed. *Apollinaire on Art: Essays and Reviews, 1902–1918.*
(Documents of 20th-Century Art ser.)
New York, Viking, 1972.

Hamilton, George Heard. *Painting and Sculpture in Europe, 1880–1940.*
(Pelican History of Art ser.)
Baltimore, Md., Penguin Books, 1967.

Steinberg, Leo. *Other Criteria: Confrontations with Twentieth-Century Art.*
New York, Oxford University Press, 1972.

Cubism

Apollinaire, Guillaume. *The Cubist Painters.* (Documents of Modern Art ser.)
New York, Wittenborn, 1962.

Barr, Alfred H., Jr. *Cubism and Abstract Art.* Reprint.
First publ. 1936. New York, Arno for The Museum of Modern Art, 1967.

Fry, Edward F. *Cubism.*
London, Thames and Hudson; New York, McGraw-Hill, 1966.

Golding, John. *Cubism: A History and an Analysis, 1907–1914.* Rev. ed.
New York, Harper and Row, 1972.

Rosenblum, Robert. *Cubism and Twentieth-Century Art.*
New York, Abrams, 1968.

Schwartz, Paul Waldo. *Cubism.*
New York, Praeger, 1971.

Georges Braque

Mullins, Edwin. *The Art of Georges Braque.*
New York, Abrams, 1968.

Ponge, Francis; Descargues, Pierre; and Malraux, André. *Georges Braque.*
New York, Abrams, 1971.

Richardson, John. *Georges Braque.*
Greenwich, Conn., New York Graphic Society, 1961.

Russell, John. *Georges Braque.*
London, Phaidon, 1959.

Juan Gris

Kahnweiler, Daniel-Henry. *Gris, His Life and Work.*
New York, Abrams, 1969.

Soby, James Thrall. *Juan Gris.*
New York, The Museum of Modern Art, New York, 1958.

Fernand Léger

Delevoy, Robert L. *Léger: Biographical and Critical Study.*
Geneva, Skira, 1962.

Fry, Edward F., ed. *Fernand Léger: The Functions of Painting.* (Documents of
20th-Century Art ser.)
New York, Viking, 1973.

Pablo Picasso

Ashton, Dore, ed. *Picasso on Art: A Selection of Views.* (Documents of
20th-Century Art ser.)
New York, Viking, 1972.

Barr, Alfred H., Jr. *Picasso: Fifty Years of His Art.* Reprint.
First publ. 1946. New York, The Museum of Modern Art, 1974.

Daix, Pierre. *Picasso.*
New York, Praeger, 1965.

Jaffé, Hans L. C. *Pablo Picasso.*
New York, Abrams, 1964.

Kahnweiler, Daniel-Henry, with Frances Crémieux. *My Galleries and Painters.*
(Documents of 20th-Century Art ser.)
New York, Viking, 1971.

Leymarie, Jean. *Picasso: The Artist of the Century.*
New York, Viking, 1972.

Rubin, William. *Picasso in the Collection of The Museum of Modern Art.*
New York, The Museum of Modern Art, 1972.

LIST OF ILLUSTRATIONS

Dimensions: height precedes width; a third dimension, depth, is given for sculptures and constructions where relevant. Foreign titles are in English, except in cases where the title does not translate or is better known in its original form. Asterisked titles indicate works reproduced in color.

Braque, Georges
(1882–1963)

Large Nude, 1907–08 (fig. 8)
Oil on canvas, 55¾ x 40 inches
Private collection, Paris

**Road near L'Estaque,* 1908 (pl. II)
Oil on canvas, 23¾ x 19¾ inches
The Museum of Modern Art, New York
Given anonymously (by exchange)

Still Life with Fruit, 1908 (fig. 11)
Oil on canvas, 26 x 21½ inches
Nationalmuseum, Stockholm

Harbor in Normandy, 1909 (fig. 12)
Oil on canvas, 32 x 21¾ inches
The Art Institute of Chicago
The Samuel A. Marx Purchase Fund and Major Acquisitions Fund

La Roche-Guyon: the Château, 1909 (fig. 13)
Oil on canvas, 31¾ x 23⅝ inches
Nationalmuseum, Stockholm

Still Life with Violin and Jug, 1909 (fig. 22)
Oil on canvas, 46¾ x 29¼ inches
Kunstmuseum, Basel

**Man with a Guitar,* 1911 (pl. V)
Oil on canvas, 45¾ x 31⅞ inches
The Museum of Modern Art, New York
Acquired through the Lillie P. Bliss Bequest

The Portuguese, 1911 (fig. 23)
Oil on canvas, 46¾ x 32½ inches
Kunstmuseum, Basel

Still Life on a Table, 1912 (fig. 27)
Collage on paper, 18½ x 24⅜ inches
Private collection, Paris

Still Life with Ace of Clubs, 1912–13 (fig. 26)
Oil and charcoal on canvas, 32¼ x 24 inches
Musée National d'Art Moderne, Paris

Still Life (with word "Vin"), 1913 (fig. 28)
Pasted-paper, pencil and wash on paper, 23⅛ x 17¼ inches
Philadelphia Museum of Art
The Louise and Walter Arensberg Collection

Musical Forms (Guitar and Clarinet), 1918 (fig. 50)
Pasted-paper, corrugated cardboard, charcoal, and gouache on cardboard, 30⅜ x 37⅜ inches
Philadelphia Museum of Art
The Louise and Walter Arensberg Collection

**Café-Bar,* 1919 (pl. XII)
Oil on canvas, 64 x 32¾ inches
Kunstmuseum, Basel

Gris, Juan
(1887–1927)

Rooftops, 1911 (fig. 33)
Oil on canvas, 20⅝ x 13½ inches
The Solomon R. Guggenheim Museum, New York

The Man in the Café, 1912 (fig. 34)
Oil on canvas, 50½ x 34⅝ inches
Philadelphia Museum of Art
The Louise and Walter Arensberg Collection

Portrait of Picasso, 1912 (fig. 35)
Oil on canvas, 29¼ x 36⅞ inches
The Art Institute of Chicago
Gift of Mr. Leigh B. Block

Grapes and Wine, 1913 (fig. 36)
Oil on canvas, 36¼ x 23⅝ inches
The Museum of Modern Art, New York
Bequest of Anna Erickson Levene in memory of her husband, Dr. Phoebus Aaron Theodor Levene

Violin and Engraving, 1913 (fig. 37)
Oil and collage on canvas, 25⅝ x 19⅝ inches
The Museum of Modern Art, New York
Bequest of Anna Erickson Levene in memory of her husband, Dr. Phoebus Aaron Theodor Levene

Playing Cards and Glass of Beer, 1913 (fig. 38)
Oil on canvas with collage, 20⅝ x 14⅜ inches
The Columbus Gallery of Fine Arts, Columbus, Ohio
Ferdinand Howald Collection

**Breakfast,* 1914 (pl. VII)
Pasted-paper over crayon and oil on canvas, 31⅞ x 23½ inches
The Museum of Modern Art, New York
Acquired through the Lillie P. Bliss Bequest

The Tea Cups, 1914 (fig. 39)
Collage, oil and charcoal on canvas, 26 x 36¾ inches
Kunstsammlung Nordrhein-Westfalen, Düsseldorf

Still Life (Bottle and Fruitdish), 1917 (fig. 48)
Oil on panel, 28¾ x 36⅛ inches
The Minneapolis Institute of Arts
The John R. Van Derlip Fund

Léger, Fernand
(1881–1955)

Table and Fruit, 1909 (fig. 41)
Oil on canvas, 33 x 38⅞ inches
The Minneapolis Institute of Arts
William Hood Dunwoody Fund

**Contrast of Forms,* 1913 (pl. X)
Oil on canvas, 39½ x 32 inches
The Museum of Modern Art, New York
Philip L. Goodwin Collection

Village in the Forest, 1914 (fig. 42)
Oil on canvas, 52 x 38¾ inches
Kunstmuseum, Basel

Picasso, Pablo
(1881–1973)

Portrait of Leo Stein, c. 1905 (fig. 18)
Ink on paper, 6¼ x 4½ inches
Philadelphia Museum of Art
The Louis E. Stern Collection

Woman Combing Her Hair, 1906 (fig. 3)
Oil on canvas, 49⅝ x 35¾ inches
The Museum of Modern Art, New York
Extended loan of the Florene May Schoenborn and Samuel A. Marx Collection

Two Nudes, 1906 (fig. 4)
Oil on canvas, 59⅝ x 36⅝ inches
The Museum of Modern Art, New York
Gift of G. David Thompson in honor of Alfred H. Barr, Jr.

Gertrude Stein, 1906 (fig. 19)
Oil on canvas, 39⅜ x 32 inches
The Metropolitan Museum of Art, New York
Bequest of Gertrude Stein, 1946

Head, 1906 (fig. 5)
Watercolor, 8⅞ x 6⅞ inches
The Museum of Modern Art, New York
John S. Newberry Collection

Head of a Man (Study for "Les Demoiselles d'Avignon"), 1907 (fig. 6)
Watercolor, 8⅞ x 6⅞ inches
The Museum of Modern Art, New York
John S. Newberry Collection

Study for "Les Demoiselles d'Avignon," 1907 (fig. 2)
Pencil and pastel, 18¾ x 25 inches
Kunstmuseum, Basel

*Les Demoiselles d'Avignon, 1907 (pl. I)
Oil on canvas, 96 x 92 inches
The Museum of Modern Art, New York
Acquired through the Lillie P. Bliss Bequest

Big Dryad, 1908 (fig. 9)
Oil on canvas, 73¼ x 42⅛ inches
The Hermitage Museum, Leningrad

Seated Nude Woman, 1908 (fig. 7)
Oil on canvas, 45¾ x 35 inches
Philadelphia Museum of Art
The Louise and Walter Arensberg Collection

Fruit Dish, 1909 (fig. 30)
Oil on canvas, 29¼ x 24 inches
The Museum of Modern Art, New York
Acquired through the Lillie P. Bliss Bequest

Still Life with Liqueur Bottle, 1909 (fig. 10)
Oil on canvas, 32⅛ x 25¾ inches
The Museum of Modern Art, New York
Mrs. Simon Guggenheim Fund

Houses on the Hill, Horta, 1909 (fig. 15)
Oil on canvas, 25⅝ x 32 inches
Private collection, New York

Factory at Horta de Ebro, 1909 (fig. 14)
Oil on canvas, 21 x 24 inches
The Hermitage Museum, Leningrad

*Woman with Pears, 1909 (pl. IV)
Oil on canvas, 36¼ x 28⅞ inches
The Museum of Modern Art, New York
Extended loan from the Florene May Schoenborn
   and Samuel A. Marx Collection

Woman's Head, 1909 (fig. 16)
Bronze, 16¼ inches high
The Museum of Modern Art, New York
Purchase

*Still Life with Bread and Fruitdish on a Table, 1909 (pl. III)
Oil on canvas, 65½ x 53 inches
Kunstmuseum, Basel

Portrait of Ambroise Vollard, 1909–10 (fig. 20)
Oil on canvas, 36¼ x 25½ inches
Pushkin Museum, Moscow

Girl with a Mandolin, 1910 (fig. 17)
Oil on canvas, 39½ x 29 inches
Private collection, New York

Female Nude, 1910–11 (fig. 21)
Oil on canvas, 38¾ x 30⅜ inches
Philadelphia Museum of Art
The Louise and Walter Arensberg Collection

"Ma Jolie" (Woman with a Zither or Guitar), 1911–12 (fig. 24)
Oil on canvas, 39⅜ x 25¾ inches
The Museum of Modern Art, New York
Acquired through the Lillie P. Bliss Bequest

Guitar, 1912 (fig. 43)
Sheet metal and wire, 30½ x 13¾ x 7⅝ inches
The Museum of Modern Art, New York
Gift of the artist

The Architect's Table, 1912 (fig. 25)
Oil on canvas, 28⅝ x 23½ inches
The Museum of Modern Art, New York
Promised gift of Mr. and Mrs. William S. Paley,
   New York

*Man with a Hat, 1912 (pl. VI)
Charcoal, ink and pasted-paper, 24½ x 18⅝ inches
The Museum of Modern Art, New York
Purchase

The Violin (Violin and Compote of Fruit), 1913 (fig. 31)
Charcoal, colored papers, gouache, and printed papers, 25¼ x 19½ inches
Philadelphia Museum of Art
The A. E. Gallatin Collection

Guitar and Wineglass, 1913 (fig. 32)
Pasted-paper and charcoal, 18⅞ x 14⅜ inches
Marion Koogler McNay Art Institute,
   San Antonio, Texas

*Guitar, 1913 (pl. VIII)
Charcoal, wax crayon, ink and pasted-paper, 26⅛ x 19½ inches
Private collection, New York

Student with a Pipe, 1913–14 (fig. 29)
Oil, charcoal, pasted-paper and sand on canvas, 28¾ x 23⅛ inches
Private collection, New York

Card Player, 1913–14 (fig. 47)
Oil on canvas, 42½ x 35¼ inches
The Museum of Modern Art, New York
Acquired through the Lillie P. Bliss Bequest

*Pipe and Musical Score, 1914 (pl. IX)
Pasted-paper, charcoal, pencil and gouache on paper, 20¼ x 26¼ inches
The Museum of Fine Arts, Houston, Texas
Gift of Mr. and Mrs. S. M. McAshan, Jr.

Glass of Absinth, 1914 (fig. 44)
Painted bronze with silver sugar strainer, 8½ x 6½ inches
The Museum of Modern Art, New York
Gift of Mrs. Bertram Smith

Glass, Newspaper and Bottle, 1914 (fig. 46)
Oil and sand on canvas, 14¼ x 24⅛ inches
The Museum of Modern Art, New York
The Sidney and Harriet Janis Collection

Still Life, 1914 (fig 45)
Painted wood with upholstery fringe, 18⅞ inches wide
The Tate Gallery, London

Still Life with Fruit, 1915 (fig. 40)
Oil on canvas, 25 x 31½ inches
The Columbus Gallery of Fine Arts, Columbus, Ohio
Ferdinand Howald Collection

*Harlequin, 1915 (pl. XI)
Oil on canvas, 72¼ x 41⅜ inches
The Museum of Modern Art, New York
Acquired through the Lillie P. Bliss Bequest

Guitar, 1919 (fig. 49)
Oil, charcoal and pinned-paper on canvas, 85 x 31 inches
The Museum of Modern Art, New York
Gift of A. Conger Goodyear

Rubens, Peter Paul
(1577–1640)

The Judgment of Paris, c. 1632–35 (fig. 1)
Oil on panel, 57⅛ x 76⅜ inches
The National Gallery, London